PRAISE FOR
GIRLHOOD
x
A HAUNTING

"Can Nancy, everyone's girl detective, finally solve the crime against generations of girls? Can she, after so many crimes solved through story, finally solve not the whodunnit (because we know who done it) but the mystery of the crime itself? That is what this somehow both gestural and capacious book dares to ask."

— Lucy Corin,
author of *The Swank Hotel*

"Jessica Rae Bergamino's *Girlhood x A Haunting* summons the girl sleuth, Nancy Drew. Bergamino's gorgeous gurlesque poems take the reader on a tour of the horrors of high school ("Her ghosts push through her school's green halls, laughing their stuffy laugh"), child abuse ("When my father corners his daughter in detail he warns her, at least, tells her, Nancy, I'm going to talk to you like a grown-up now, treat you like one, break the glass of my anger and let it evergreen in you, all myrtle and clove"), and trauma ("where your memory splits from sight"). True crime is popular because viewing violation provides the illusion of control in a culture where so many are unsafe. Bergamino's book channels one of the OG feminist icons of the genre and empowers readers to navigate, perhaps even survive, the true crimes of childhood. I love this book."

— Claudia Cortese,
author of *Wasp Queen*

"If you like your true crime, noir, and haunted house to have a little tongue in their cheek, bite in their bark, and redemption in their existential dread Jessica Rae Bergamino's *Girlhood x A Haunting* is for you. It may also be about you. Were you, too, the queer dark-haired daughter—mouth stuffed with nails, body stuffed with brittle noise—of a conman and a bitter hiccup? Whose best friend, laughing like a silver bell, loved the worst men? Whose doctor flipped girl flesh inside out trying to disprove her mystery? Can you remember, yet? If it was anything like that, unbury yourself, Nancy. Look for me and [I] will look for you. And if it was nothing like that? Buckle-up buttercup. Golly and gasp, the poet rises from ash!"

— Danielle Pafunda,
author of *Along the Road Everyone Must Travel*
(winner of the Saturnalia Books 2023 Poetry Prize)

"In girlhood, survival is not guaranteed. If you've had a girlhood you know this. It is a mystery to be solved. Because every brutal moment works to take that girl away, physically, psychologically. In Jessica Rae Bergamino's brilliant and harrowing, raw and intimate *Girlhood x A Haunting*, survival has a name. It's Nancy. And Nancy knows that survival is 'a grief she's tumbling towards' because 'surviving means seeing everything.' Nancy knows that to survive is to 'Steal the body back'."

— EJ Colen,
author of *What Weaponry* and *The Green Condition*

"Forget clues—the poems in *Girlhood x A Haunting* confront a new kind of investigation. How do you solve the mystery of a body when the body is your own? Through Bergamino's signature and skilled voice, balanced formal tension, and adroit cross-examination of both history and memory, these poems build a new mythology for the queer detective work required of so many of us. Urgent, evocative, and, indeed, haunting, Bergamino has collected Nancy Drew and put her to work on the most vital of missions: self-reclamation. No other poet writing today could handle this case so deftly or with such clever care."

— Meg Day,
author of *Last Psalm at Sea Level*

GIRLHOOD
X
A HAUNTING

JESSICA RAE BERGAMINO

DRIFTWOOD PRESS

Independently published by *Driftwood Press*
in the United States of America.

Managing Poetry Editor & Interviewer: Sara Moore Wagner
Poetry Editor: Christen Noel Kauffman & Ben Kline
Cover Image: Ío Wuerich
Cover Design: Sally Franckowiak
Interior Design: James McNulty
Fonts: Knockout, Merriweather, & Alternate Gothic Extra Condensed

Copyright © 2024 by Jessica Rae Bergamino
All Rights Reserved.

No part of this publication
may be reproduced, stored in a retrieval
program, or transmitted, in any form or by
any means (electronic, mechanical,
photographic, recording, etc.), without
the publisher's written permission.

First published February 25, 2025
ISBN-13: 978-1-949065-34-3

Please visit our website at www.driftwoodpress.com
or email us at editor@driftwoodpress.net.

CONTENTS

THE RESCUE	27
THE MISSING WILL	31
AN UNPLEASANT MEETING	35
RACING THE STORM	38
A SURPRISING STORY	42
AN EXCITING APPOINTMENT	46
THE ANGRY DOG	48
A FORGOTTEN SECRET	53
HELPFUL DISCLOSURES	58
FOLLOWING A CLUE	60
AN UNEXPECTED ADVENTURE	63
A DESPERATE SITUATION	66
THE FRUSTRATING WAIT	72
A TENSE CHASE	80
NANCY'S RISKY UNDERTAKING	82
STRANGE INSTRUCTIONS	86
A SUSPENSEFUL SEARCH	89
STARTLING REVELATIONS	92
A HAPPY FINALE	97
INTERVIEW: A SPELL FOR UNDERSTANDING WHERE THE STORY ENDS AND WHERE I BEGIN	103

Extinguish me from this.
I was sixteen for twenty years. By September I will be a ghost.

— Lucie Brock-Broido, "A Girl Ago"

The plots of Nancy Drew mysteries are like sonnets,
endless variations on an inflexible form.

— Bobbie Ann Mason, *The Girl Sleuth*

I do not yet have the mental courage to be only I.

— Helene Cixous, *The Book of Promethea*

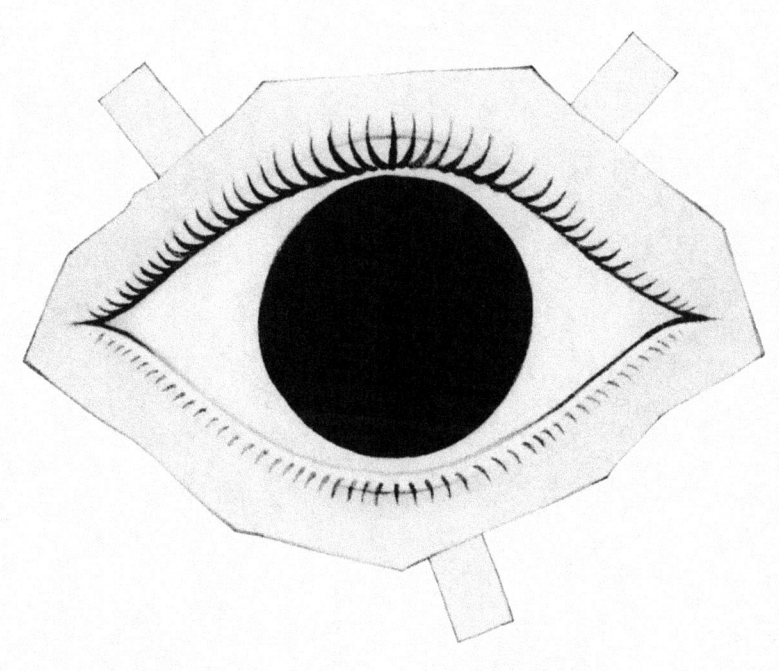

[[[

I unburied myself from the echo of her, carved girl flesh from her lemon rind breath.

Trance of bone, my body is as pure as fiction –

]]]

My [I] thins in the menace of light.
Unsolid. Unsoiled.
A girl is a girl is a girl.
Is subtext.
Is colony quivering towards collapse.
Memory picks at itself like carrion.

I mean I [I] like dandruff.
I mean I [I] like a dressing gown.

I mean

~~I'll tell you the truth if you promise~~

Pen¹ (pen) *n.* an instrument for writing or drawing with ink or similar fluid

Pen¹ (pen) *trans verb.* to write or compose with a pen

Pen² (pen) *n.* a fenced enclosure for animals; the animals kept in such an enclosure

Pen³ (pen) *n.* a female swam [orig. unknown]

Pen⁴ (pen) *n.* a penitentiary

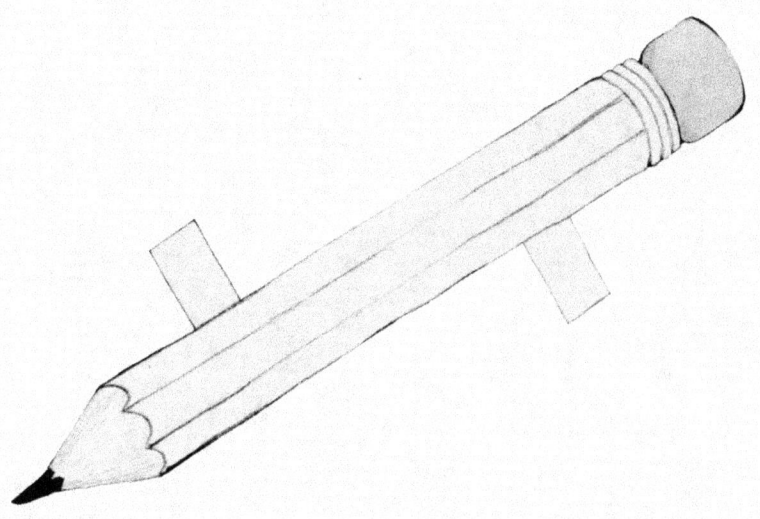

Nancy tells people more than they need to know. Her name is past tense, *Drew* instead of *Draw*. She's transitive, always already happened and happening, always already the train in the station and the crayon untipped on thin pink paper. She's not very tall but she's outgrown the weeds. Her bones are blown, her knees are rough and scabbed. She waves herself goodbye from the platform, choking on the engine's steam. Her lips are chapped, her mouth is stuffed with nails. Her pretty blouses strain against their pearls.

Or, she assumes she is a window, her curtains pulled and driven from the shine. She keeps missing herself, her reflection torn from freckled hips where bruises never bloom beyond her panties. Dear escape, Nancy is looking for your fire. She's the well and the girl at the bottom, the rope and the throwing arm. She knows girls are just codes waiting to be cracked, parentheses that must be filled. Nancy digs her unsteady heels into the ground. She dyes her hair blond because her father says it will make him love her more, or, maybe, better.

[[[

I imagine how we slip in and out of one another,

                 untestedasammunition.

      Parallel lines drawn yellow on the same unmapped road.

  There is a you I remember and a me I forget.

         One day, everyone will love you.

 & me?

        I rock your chin in my cradle and squeeze.

]]]

When you wake, you're the scene of her crime.

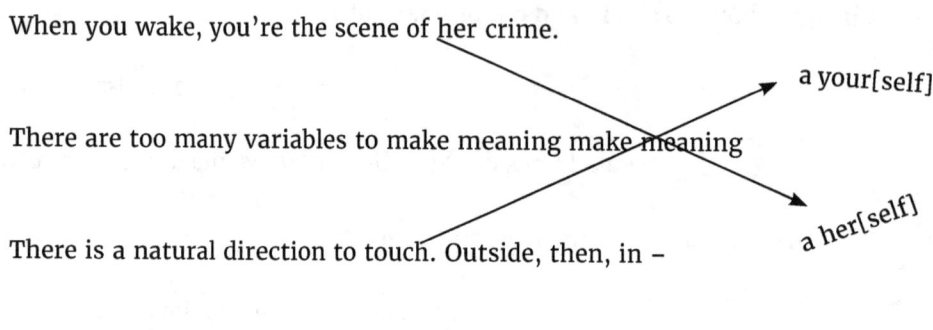

There are too many variables to make meaning make meaning

There is a natural direction to touch. Outside, then, in –

[I] seizes her (a bird in her throat).

She's been told she shouldn't speak until spoken to, but her body aches with brittle noise. Something curves through her, undoing the voice from the corners of her mouth. It must be a ghost!, her father teases over dinner, reaching for his daughter's cheek. Stopping short.

[[[

Every Nancy is a Jessica and every Jessica is a Nancy.
We fold each other in and out of laundry baskets

that bear the burden of our doubled life. Shame leaks out,
permanent as ink, but nothing is too dangerous for girls.

Still, [I] worries at her through the walls, unhooking time
from tender, fat from salt. We have no terms for surrender.

 & even lies become memories, so untangle the facts.
[I] had a father for twenty years before he disappeared.
No forwarding tether. No address.
When he risked, he risked everything.
When he lost, he lost hard.
Girls were always falling in the road in front of him.
They disappeared before he hit them, but the day was never saved.
His headlights snatched the shine from their hair.
Quarters silver into slots, dollars vanish into dealers' hands.
His checks were signed with Nancy's name.

& [I] had a mother, once, but she's gone too.
Replaced by a hiccup / a housedress / a mirror / a mimic, unmade – /
She's stolen all the keys from the locks, jams her eye
in every empty hole. She's forced the mirrors to window,
stripped the silver from their backs.
It shines beneath her fingernails and snatches
shards of light where her teeth should be.
Her aprons cower in the closet. Her skin slumbers loose
along her bones. She screws her eyes into every door.
She watches. She waits. She teaches the way love
springs from the back of a hand.

[1] For the purposes of this investigation, we'll call her Hannah.

& there's so much [I] cannot name for you
because it's been taken from me. Whole years

lost to the calendars that made them & [I] is trapped
in the slippage between past and tense. Days trickle away

and [I] is wary of the meaning of absence.

Two memories stitched from fiction.

One is a girl-shaped doll made from husks and skins and stains and spit.

The other is dead because [I] murdered her.

I'm sorry, Nancy.
I'm stealing a second self from you.
I'm gambling on your pluck.
So be brave, Nancy. Please.
Be braver than [I] can be.

A clever girl, Nancy makes a decision. She'll play the role of detective, will approach her body as both the mystery and the clue. She'll separate herself from herself like the shell from the yolk, like the truth from the dare. The villains will be obvious, easy to find. She'll know love scented soft as an old book with ribbons curling down the spine. She studies her lines in the mirror, practices her measured golly and gasp.

So go wild, girl sleuth. Go proof.
Go follow the ghosts that follow you,
that trick your luck and suck
your crooked teeth.

Decode the message sent
from another version of yourself,
your name unstitched by the rough hands
that left you gnawing there.

THE RESCUE

Nancy is wise in the ways of subterfuge. She knows loose lips sink ships and open car doors. When her father is happy he's very happy, but when he's sad he's very sad. He disappears and everyone tells Nancy it's because she's been bad. Bad girl!, they say. You're doing it wrong! She can't pull herself from her own hat or uncuff her wrists at will, so she cuts off her hands instead. She sets traps in the field and catches her own lucky foot. She holds her breath, drowning in her own stench. She skins her twitching body to find the hollow space within.

Without his briefcase or shoe polish, her father is fool's gold flaunting fake shine. One day he's calling every dealer by name, cards wilting in his eager hands. The next, he's a magician cutting a woman in half, his mustache oiled and curled. He stuffs her mouth with roaches and moths, holds his daughter hostage in the mirror. The audience doesn't know if they should vomit or applaud. Charlatan! Fraud! He cocks his gun and tries to meet himself half way. His grief is the cover of a magazine where Nancy is naked and his ghosts pour out from between her spread legs. She is a modern girl and the magazine is tasteful as her hair.

Hannah climbs over the body to pour another glass of wine. Another mess for her to clean. Why doesn't Nancy listen? Stubborn girl, she's always trying to prove something. She's good at history but poor at math, knows spook is just another word for spy. She dots her [I]s and they watch her through the Os. She divides herself by herself until there is still no answer. Her bed is never made but her door is always open. She never learned to turn the lock.

If she can't disappear completely, she'll climb into herself until she can steer steady in her own reflection. She'll cut away the dirty parts until her thighs are sticky with the blood.

A MISSING WILL

She sits naked on the examination table while the doctor presses his fingers in her soft and vulnerable parts. He cups Nancy's chin in his leaden hand and jams his tongue depressor tight inside her mouth. Why doesn't she want to be beautiful? Another mystery to be solved! He writes her weight on the back of a receipt, sucks his scabby lips. He gives Nancy back her bra, watches her scoop her stretch-marked breasts into the floral cups. He draws a gold star in her file and presses a sticker against her unbuttoned blouse, his thumb drawing a rough line from pink scar to pink scar.

Why doesn't she want to be beautiful? What good would it do? Her lace is indistinguishable from her stupid mouth. She never learned to shoot a gun. In the waiting room, Hannah slaps her face. Nancy gathers the stings in her palm, places them in a vase on her dresser. She arranges them to block the mirror's sight, each one an open hand reaching towards an absent sun. Where are your panties? Hannah asks, pulling off Nancy's dress.

When you become a girl detective, the morning tide salts your veins into an open hum. It rises with every hunch, flooding the hidden staircases you've carved inside your breath. Nancy keenly regards the stranger who sums her up in the mirror. She knows water is only ice for as long as it hesitates, that escape is only an option for lovelier girls. Outside, layers of green make way for the thrills of light. Birds stutter their nests empty. Traffic stumbles in the distance.

[[[

Have courage, Nancy.
[I] can only promise you'll survive.

AN UNPLEASANT MEETING

Her ghosts push through her school's green halls, laughing their stuffy laugh. They trail her to the bathroom stalls where she steels herself to burn. At lunch, they lift her friend Helen's hem with their mist, exposing her thighs to the cafeteria's glare. Her friend doesn't seem to notice, laughing like a silver bell in Ned's steady arms. Nancy doesn't blame her. Prom queen. Captain of whatever. She covers her face with her hands and listens for the waiting sea. The ghosts lick the salt from her lips.

She imagines their bodies moving together, wondering at their lack of symmetry, at how they coil and flex. Where they grow hard. Where they grow soft. Where she might fold herself inside their velvet hum. When she and Helen talk on the phone each night, cords twisted around their fingers, she falls asleep inside the hollow of her friend's floral breath. They were always like this, she thinks, two halves of different wholes. A peach splitting soft at the seam. A plum caught in a wolf's teeth. But Nancy, O, Nancy, are you paying attention?

She can never remember getting to class, seems to skip the bus stop and the locker door's tinny clang, but Helen is a hundred well-laid plans in calendar entries of clear, curled script kept with ease. She softens her hands against Nancy's back, brushing the ghosts from her shoulders. They crunch beneath her well-meaning shoes. She tells Nancy she's a lucky girl / a roof over her head girl / a middle-class girl. She dots her eyes and crosses her ankles, but Nancy knows neither are the protective spells she wants them to be. So try harder, Nancy! Stop making things up! Squint and see the bodies made of ether that pierce and prick you to pieces.

RACING THE STORM

Nancy finds what's left of Hannah scattered on the floor like autumn leaves, ghosts fumbling her dress off her shoulders, staining her blue as a vein. She unfolds herself until there's nothing left and the room smells like arsenic and rosemary. Nancy fishes in her purse and offers a compact, wise Nancy who knows how to cover a bruise, but no, Hannah brushes Nancy's hand away, your father doesn't like it when I wear makeup, except when he's holding me down, etcetera, etcetera, etc&.

When my father corners his daughter in detail he warns her, at least, tells her, Nancy, I'm going to talk to you like a grown-up now, treat you like one, break the glass of my anger and let it evergreen in you, all myrtle and clove. Hannah isn't so lucky. She's the servant and the mess, the mistress and the maid. Nancy dusts the fingerprints from her wrist, measures what's left of her white wine pulse.

Where does she go, leaving her skin behind to collect her dust?
Is she tattered like lace?
Does she know annihilation is not the same as love?

						A woman waiting to be solved.
						 A puzzle aching for a clue.
					A grief Nancy knows she's tumbling towards.

She stands up and sighs the wrinkles from her skirt,
leaving Hannah to sort herself from the safety pins she's drowning in.

"Dad?" Nancy called quickly.

There was no answer, but from somewhere in the shadows came the sound of heavy breathing.

A SURPRISING STORY

Rage is fat in Nancy's mouth. The doctor calls it her tongue, but she calls it precision. It has poise. Purpose. Collateral. He asks her what she's thinking and she says he feels like a graveyard in winter where the geese are flocking in their down. He tells her girls are wild animals desperate to be controlled. He tells her he hates her smell. She has no reason to be afraid. He loves her like a daughter. He puts her on a diet. He counts backwards and she closes her eyes, waiting for the familiar drop of darkness to cover her body with its curtain.

The mold is broken. Pattern unblocked. I remember his balding head, wire rim glasses, his office in the basement of his house with the white noise machine whirring beside the laundry. It smelled like mold, wet leather, summer stink.
He had a daughter with facets like a shopping list:
Queer.
Fat.
Brunette.
Bespeckled.
Estranged.

The conversation went like this:

Him: "'I need you to know that I'm experiencing counter-transference.'"

Someone, please, translate that to girl.
Make it make sense. Erase his fingerprints from my bedroom window.

Sometimes it hurts from the outside in, sometimes it spills the other way. She wants to hem herself into another pattern, one where her dresses fit and she has a mother to shoo the ghosts away, but the clever detective knows she deserves what she's been given. She counts the ceiling's water stains, keeps her smart mouth shut. She empties herself of herself, just like Hannah who sees everything except the men who claim Nancy as their own.

Nancy, it's been twenty years and my thighs are still caught on that fake leather chair. I wish I could protect you from all of this, but I need you to solve this mystery. I need you to tell me what happened to me. I need to let it crash inside your throat because I can't keep letting it curdle in mine. That voice inside my body. I don't know why it is the moment that feels like you could undrop the spindle and unprick your finger. Maybe some part of me was always looking for you. Now I'll make you look for me.

AN EXCITING APPOINTMENT

A car honks in her driveway and Nancy runs to greet it, her shoes clickity-clacking beneath her fur. Venus of the cigarette smoke, she pours from the house in her too-short skirt with her blouse half undone. The radio is loud as Helen's body and Ned's hand is halfway up her thigh. Nancy bites her lip, pretending she doesn't see, but the girl sleuth knows surviving means seeing everything.

Helen and Nancy arrive, but where's Ned gone? Did the car drive itself? Helen shrugs her pimpled shoulders. He always comes back, little lost dog. There's no mystery here! It's Friday night and Helen drags Nancy into the mall's unforgiving light, leading her friend from store to store as she dissolves like sugar in her palm. Nancy applauds each dress stretched tight beneath Helen's smirk, wanting to say something darling or daring or bright. Nothing beautiful comes in Nancy's size, but Helen doesn't seem to mind. They're good girls, unfortunate girls, and with Ned nowhere to be found she presses Nancy against the dressing-room wall, her hands on her hips and their mouths full of gasp.

THE ANGRY DOG

Rage is fat in Nancy's mouth. Her doctor says he'll pick her up at school after the last bell, then laughs, says he's kidding, only kidding, she should learn to take a joke. It curdles in Nancy's stomach, feels like color of corn in autumn: wild and pecked upon the stalk. She tries to forget because names should protect the innocent. She aches to be as repulsive as she feels, desperate to trap herself in meaning. Her diary is open on his desk, coffee-ringed and finger-stained.

Without a treasure map or code to crack, she risks drowning in the flood of her own shame. She makes herself the escape route, shimmying down the secret passage of her throat into her warm, waiting belly. She rests in the chair she's made herself there, tends herself safe from the fire. The curtains are open. There are flowers in the vase. Ghosts are never linear. The other Nancies slip in and out of speech in the next room.

She wants to compare the original to the revision, to understand where the story went astray. Her memory ends where her diary begins, ink unspooling in bruises on her dimpled thighs. She chases herself through herself, watches her ripe and lonely body disappear through an open window. Is she a now or a then? A here or a becoming? A girl or just a memory of meat? A mystery Nancy doesn't need to solve. One divided by One is still One, a stalemate still a draw.

Nancy opens her eyes. When had she closed them? The doctor is screaming. She should be ashamed for teasing him with her soft and violent parts. He says she's bad for running her mouth / her fingers through her hair / that she's a selfish girl / spoiled girl / bad girl / stupid fat slut. He says he loves her. He calls her by his daughter's name.

Tomorrow, the guidance counselor will turn him away from the school's double doors.

A FORGOTTEN SECRET

Did rise. Did tear along.
Did carry the sour heave of memory.
Did fold my body upon the pillow's curve,
did teach myself to pray. Did pray. Did sleep.
Did choir an echo to swell through time.
Did pocket watch, did compass.
Did whisper a girl from the silence of ghost.
Did travel on the folded map to the roaring inside.

Did see myself smaller, at least, stranger,
where the hinge of losing
had not yet become loss.
Did vein, did hollow in light,
did hold my own chapped hand.
Did hair, did makeup, did tenderly
press pigment upon my broken lip.
Did stutter. Did slur. Did shush
my open mouth, the empty glove.
Did grace, did dare, did learn the ways
forgiveness is the heaviest thing to dare.

Did grieve. Did grief. Did check the weather,
choose the sweater, did patch the jeans
with holes along the seam. Did purchase,
did pressure, did put the safety on the scissors.
Did shuttle myself away, did haunt,
did swallow a tongue of sweat
formed on the belly of a forgotten glass.

Did ice, did block, did measure the doing.
Did carry. Did return. Did mother. Did father.
Did slumber, did speak. Did suck blood
from the bitten nail, the thumb that bruised.
Did wash the dirt-stained sheets.
Did take the pills. Did not take the pills.
Cut the story from my own matted hair.

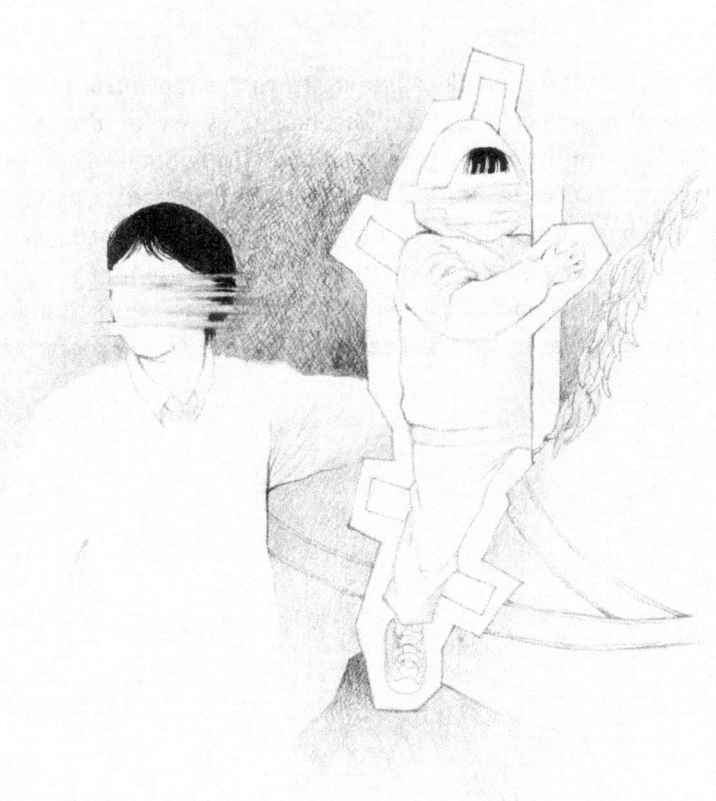

He caught Nancy roughly by the arm.

"Think you're smart, eh?" he snarled. "Well, I'm smarter!"

Nancy struggled to get away. She twisted and squirmed, kicked and clawed. But she was helpless in the vicelike grip of the powerful man.

HELPFUL DISCLOSURES

She could be unfastened like a garter, a swoon slipped from skin. She could be the perfect daughter, the boiling water or the pot that nevers. Me? I'm little more than a shiver; I carry myself red as any other meat. Luck strummed my cats from cradles, sung my cupboards bare. I learned to be rampant as onions in spring, violent as they said I was. Like a good crime scene, I was temporary. Open-mouthed with evidence, I hunted for new ways to perform my body as the swindle that it was. Bad seeds spilled out of me, coarse across the bed.

Girl was just a detour on the way to ghost. I am my father's daughter. This virus churns between us. Please love me despite the things you've said I've done.

FOLLOWING A CLUE

Nancy stands in the kitchen in her pajamas, her legs bare, her hair nested like a little girl's. Her father sits at the table as if he never learned to blast, but Nancy knows more than people tell her. She knows some men are made to disappear, that some girls are just animals pacing in their ruts. She knows when her father is happy he is very happy and when he is sad he is very sad. She knows he wants to win something more than he's earned, has always played a minor part in someone else's film. He sells the leading man a newspaper and shines his shoes in Technicolor, or lights a cigarette in front of the black and white bar. Stock markets crash and men don't always float to the surface. His lines come from a can:

As far back as I can remember, I always wanted to be a gangster.

REVENGE IS A DISH THAT TASTES BEST WHEN SERVED COLD

I NEVER FUCKED ANYBODY OVER IN MY LIFE THAT DIDN'T HAVE IT COMING TO THEM.

I'M GOINT TO MAKE HIM AN OFFER HE CAN'T REFUSE.

There's ways of killing yourself without killing yourself.

great men are not born great, they grow great.

YOU CAN'T FUCK THE FUTURE. THE FUTURE FUCKS YOU. IT CATCHES UP WITH YOU AND IT FUCKS YOU IF YOU AIN'T PLANNED FOR IT.

Nancy, you think you're the heroine, plucky and lucky and bright, but you're just a bomb that's waiting to go off, a light waiting to fuse itself to shadow. He shows her his hands and folds them in his lap.

AN UNEXPECTED ADVENTURE

Nancy gathers hunches in the full moon of her belly the way a bluejay scavenges for winter. She names the good weight intuition, understands you can't spell *confidence* without *con*. The trail of clues ends at her bedroom door, but she knows what waits inside. The bees inside her chest begin their honeyed quake.

When she thinks her mirror is asleep in its thin tin frame she lets herself linger in front of it. Her eyes flash and then deaden to a pan. *I'm Nancy*, she says, admiring the way her pink lips stretch and then pout around her name. She calculates a list of things that don't have keys: the liquor cabinet, her diary, her roller skates, her bedroom door. With her blouse unbuttoned she lifts and drops her breasts, measures her stomach's sag and lift. *Yes*, she smiles, practicing the way her doctor told her to, *yes*, he told her *yes*, she would enjoy it, *yes*, be a good girl, *yes*, behave, *yes*, *Hello*, she says, *I'm Nancy, Hello*, and her lips make the *o* and she is the *o* and the *n*'s are scattered in the dry brown grass outside her bedroom window.

She tries to be brave as a lily, biting her lips until they disappear from her muzzled face. She knows freshwater runs towards the sea, sucking cedar and sage and soft sown lettuces from their roots, all of it bellowing to be swallowed whole. Nancy longs for the rush but never the gratitude of surrender. She sleeps in the pearls that scatter across her sweater from her broached neck. When she wakes, she wakes in puddles and wonders where the water stormed from.

A DESPERATE SITUATION

Her father stands at the foot of his daughter's bed, backlit by morning. Wake up, the page-torn man whispers, shaking his daughter's ankle like a leash. Wake up, Nancy, wake up. The blanket is too thin. Everything has its cost. Nancy opens her eyes with the slow blur of an engine warming through the fields. He is unslicked for the weekend, coffee mugs milky and warm in his hands. Nancy, O Nancy, he's practically singing, we're going for a drive.

No time to do her hair, Nancy has tied her titian coif in a tasteful ribbon. Her father reaches out to stroke her cheek, stops himself with a lusty laugh. His little girl keeps growing up. Sometimes she can almost remember why she loves him. What it means to be loved.

Nancy, this is the risk of coming from somewhere.
Of not knowing how to untend the fire, unbreak the mirror.
Inheritance of slot machines. Inheritance of ash.

Maybe some mysteries can't be solved.
Maybe when dusk settles
on an untended field
it's only the beginning of night.

& at the end of a long drive through sunlight tattered leaves, another doctor tells Nancy that she's sad, but not sad enough. Stupid girl, can't she do anything right?

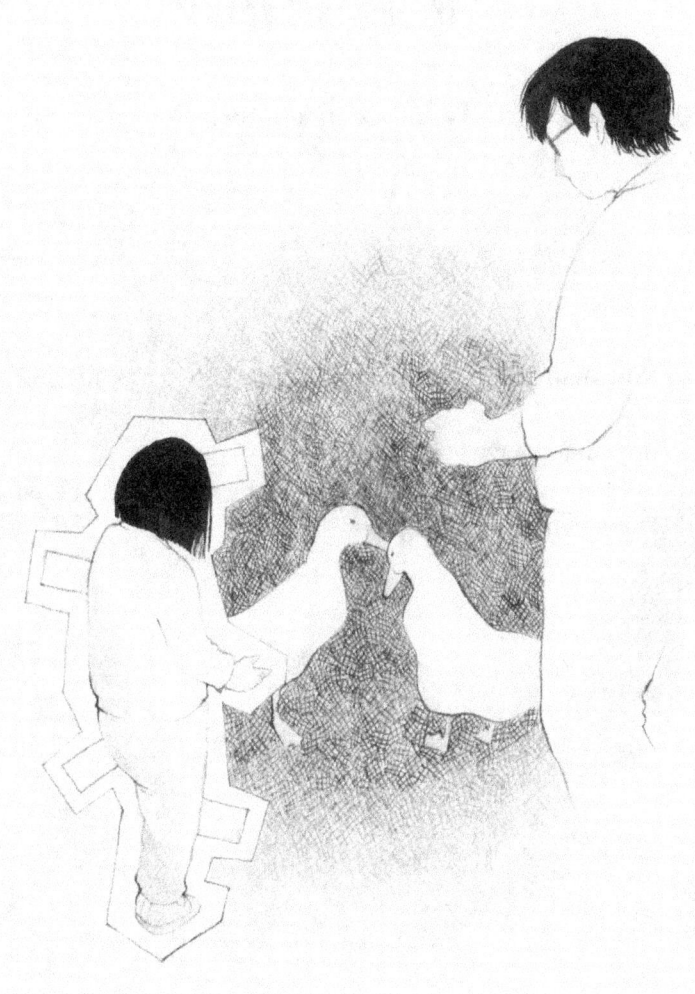

Sheer panic took possession of the girl detective.
Something very strange was going on!
She must not be caught in a trap!

THE FRUSTRATING WAIT

Q: What do you call a collection of Nancies?

A. A giggle
B. A gaggle
C. A phantom
D. A gasp

Q: How many Nancies does it take to change a lightbulb?

A. How many have you got?
B. One to hold the ladder, one to turn the bulb, one to be ashamed
C. There is no such thing as a Nancy

Q: What happened to the doctor?

A: One day I came home from school and my step-mother was laughing on the couch. She said that the doctor had been arrested for practicing without a license. Oh! I said. What a funny joke!

Q: What was she like?

A. She had no teeth
B. She wore expensive perfume
C. Most days she didn't leave the house
D. All of the above

**Q: What happens to the girl /
when the woman arrives?**

A. The ghost rattles around the hunch
of her body, tight as a fist in a wall.

A flower opens like a mouth, anemic
as a period. Trade wishes for sulfur,

transpose girlhood on to girlhood:
find the one that got away —

B. [I] w/couldn't know

Q: Were you always a Jessica?

A: Who hasn't been a Jessica?

Q: What happened to your mother?

A: Florida

Q: Why do you hunger?

A: In the dream, the doctor enters the room and I am strapped to the bed. He parts my legs and pushes aside a dirty dressing gown, draws his scalpel down the seam of my thigh. There is no blood. Only bees. They swarm the room, a thick cloud of mischief and grief. And suddenly, I am gone —

Q: What do you make within the field of loss?

A. I believe he was very sick.
B. I believe he loved me the best that he knew how.
C. I believe I don't need to forgive him any of it.
D. All of the above.
E. None of the above.

Q: Which him?

A: _____.

A TENSE CHASE

A thread unravels from Nancy's hem, stumbling her story from dollhouse to dollhouse. She follows where the thread goes, running faster and faster to keep up with it. Goodbye, good girl dresses, goodbye, ironed blouse. Goodbye, golden locket, goodbye, lucid thought. Goodbye report cards, goodbye Friday nights at the mall. Goodbye, bedtime stories, goodbye bedtime prayers. Goodbye, Sunday dinners, goodbye, garlic breath. Goodbye, goodbye, inheritance.

The road is rough and full of gravel that burrows in her sag when she falls. Above her head, ghosts spill from telephone wires, chirping and rattling the wind. The thread pulls her over potholes, keeps tangling her ankles. Nancy feels more brave than modest, more stubborn than bright. The night makes her want to touch everything, to feel the fir and sap raise against her spine. She doesn't fold her arms over her chest when headlights catch her in their glare, glaze her up and down. She catches the shine in her teeth and licks her bloody lips.

NANCY'S RISKY UNDERTAKING

Every time Nancy runs away she shakes herself from dream with nothing but quarters in her dirty palms. How queer, she muses, how unassembled I must seem, my skirt torn, my cardigan inside out. But Nancy, O, Nancy, what happened to your hair? A halo formed of ash. Nancy, O, Nancy, what happened to your teeth? She claps her fat mouth closed. She has enough bus fare to get somewhere soon. A phone rings in the nearby booth. Help is on the way. The ghosts scramble to attention.

Nancy cools in George's shadow, tries to mirror her new friend's swagger and tough. Beside them, Bess is an arrow on a map away from a place Nancy doesn't know how to leave. She loves her bubblegum breath and the way she doesn't treat being soft like punishment for being bad. Nancy's tired of the deviled eggs, of walking on the shells. The longer she stands with them the further Helen falls behind. Soon? She'll disappear completely. Nancy is jealous of the ease which she arches to whisp and smoke.

She unknots her fingers from her hem and pulls the cigarette straight from George's mouth. She inhales like a new beginning but exhales like a hag. Courage unclasps, and then? When they complain about their mothers she counts the scuffs on her shoes, dragging her toe from crack to helpless crack.

She watches George cradle Bess in her strong arms, lets the warmth flush her through and through. Poor Nancy! Always the third wheel, never brave enough to drive. Her friends don't seem to mind. The clues pour from her skirt. Her spyglass is heavy beside the tampons in her purse. Bess smiles and reaches to stroke Nancy's hair, whispering her name.

STRANGE INSTRUCTIONS

Nancy has faced many mysteries, but her body remains the biggest one. She draws off her sweater, ignoring the shivers that trample her through. She examines her breasts in the mirror, holding them up and out, wondering at their weight in her small hands. How strange, she thinks coolly, how unlike herself! She bends down to watch them hang, presses her fingers into the crease of her stomach. She still isn't what her father wants her to be, is still covered in soft dark fur. She drops her skirt to the floor and studies the way her thighs give rise to her hips, how bird-pecked they are, how frightening. How strange to see clearly where she ends and begins, to understand where she opens and how she closes. To feel that even this can be solved. She lets out a long, high wail that shakes the windows in their sills.

& I apprenticed myself to the sound
of my own name —

tried to know it as a peach knows
its fuzz —

skirt to skirt, hem to hem,
a paperdoll of meaning

as if I could remember myself
past this ending,

could storm the future to future,
autumn to fall —

— & it was twenty years before I could be
a Jessica again,

twenty years of unhooking myself
from myself,

aspiring to make myself a woman
when I wanted

to go on a girl forever —

Whole months give way to absence.
Brew tea, read cards, apostrophe &
Prozac: all of this, all of this, all of this.

Bright nothing, I release myself from you.

A SUSPENSEFUL SEARCH

A Nancy is missing from my collection of Nancies. She's unsilked the cord that bundles her selves together / given herself the slip / darted towards danger like any other paper doll. O Nancy, what were you thinking? A mystery is just a flimsy excuse for a girl. Get a life! Get a clue! Force your flashlight into the dark places where your memory splits from sight. Steal the body back.

She peels off her gloves, then her skin beneath them. The missing Nancy isn't in the stain on her shirt or the laundry basket, nor in the trap her father set for her. She isn't gagged and bound in Ned's backseat or tied, ankles to wrists, in George's trunk. She looks beneath the bed, but all she finds are dirty panties. No point checking in the closet. Her dresses are all swollen on the floor.

Nancy recoiled. The man stood in the shadows of the shrubbery so that she could not see his face directly. But at the sound of his voice she instantly knew she was in danger.

STARTLING REVELATIONS

George's blue convertible feels like a shiver of what life could be if the light bent differently around her. Maybe she would be in the driver's seat, whisking her friends off to adventure in nearby towns. People would wave hello and glass bottles of milk would be delivered to her garden stoop. Maybe she would even be beautiful enough for love. Instead, the ghosts follow them like wedding ribbons and cans, clattering the present back into tense.

When Bess presses her fingers in George's palm, something inside Nancy aches the way a fir shivers silver before a storm, needless and brutal in its sap. She wants to climb back inside herself, to curl her hair and play the pretty song, but someone has locked the door. How queer! She dusts the crumbs from her untidy frock.

They spin. They bottle. They truth. They dare. Bess dances to the radio. Breath soft, she shines. & Nancy wants to shine too, she tries so damned hard, but who can tell if the music comes from inside of her or out. She watches George and Bess tend each other like swans, flashing in and out of focus.

The tides in her chest rush through, the foam true and overwhelming as the Atlantic. The wind easts, then wests between them. Impatient George taps her fingers gaily against the steering wheel, but no, no, that isn't it at all. All the brave and fearful Nancies tremble in static as the air around them thickens to gauze.

For a long time, Jessica thought she couldn't write herself without a Nancy. That a Nancy could be better blooming without her. Is a Nancy the key or is a Nancy the lock? How is a Jessica supposed to know? Nancy, I'm afraid to find the words to replace you. I've lived inside you for so long I can't remember where your story ends and mine begins. You'll have to try to save the day another way. But wake up, Nancy! Wake up! You're drowning!

A HAPPY FINALE

When George leaves Nancy at the foot of her driveway, the hair stands up on her sturdy arms. Nancy sees everything, but says nothing. What girl isn't desperate to be loved? She waves goodbye and turns towards the mailbox with its bent little flag. The door creaks under the pressure of collection notices, one after the other, each red-stamped and confidential. But at the bottom of the pile? A letter with her name written in soft curls and ribbon. It smells like girls after a campfire. What is it?, Hannah asks from the living room, but a minor character never gets the last line. Nothing, Nancy replies. Nothing. It's mine.

It's nice to have something of her own that no one else can see. Lying in bed with the letter balanced on her chest, she watches it rise and fall with her hermit crab breath. The envelope is sealed with someone else's spit, and when Nancy tears she feels something inside her crack open. Dear Nancy, it says, Dear, Dearest, it says, and the sun is warm and her palms are honest in their sweat. Come out from your hiding, Nancy. Come out from the cracks in your ribs. Dear Nancy, O, Nancy, we have been waiting to write your name into our books of blooming.

When Nancy is ready, she folds her smartest suit in to her knapsack. A bus ticket is already pinned in the pocket of her bright green jacket with the crisp collar. Her roots have browned their way through the blonde; outside, the trees are changing colors, bowing gracefully from their yellow spines. Time is moving forward at its good and rightful pace. She's off to find her missing Nancy, ready to restore herself to the rightful order of things. The next mystery is barely a flicker in her eye.

She locks her bedroom door,
dutifully ignoring the ghost's applause.

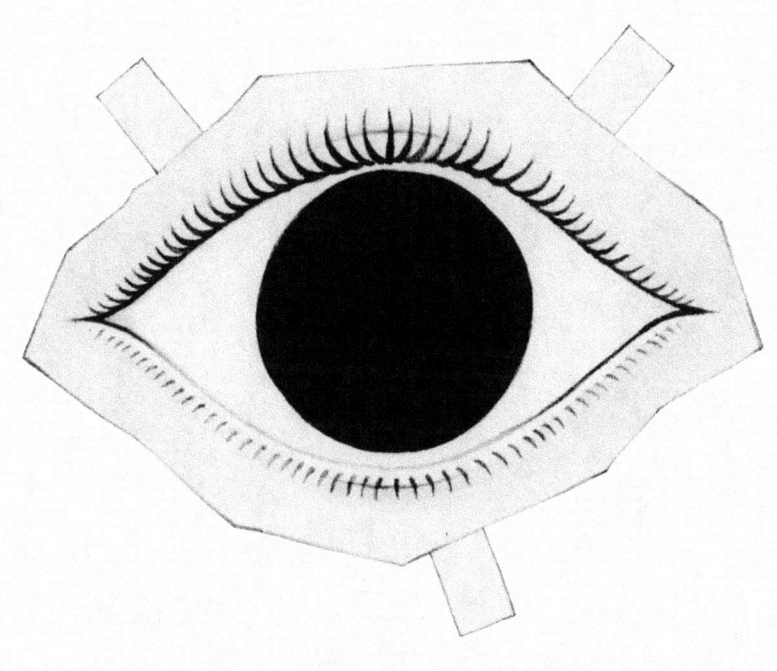

A SPELL FOR UNDERSTANDING WHERE THE STORY ENDS AND WHERE I BEGIN
A Conversation between Jessica Rae Bergamino and Sara Moore Wagner

Jessica, I was so excited to read your collection and to choose it as my first official pick for the Editor's Prize! I was not alone in this choice. All of our editors voted a resounding *yes*! I know we were pulled in even from the first epigraphs, which nod to the spectrality and the Nancy Drew content that awaits us as readers, but also that "I" mentioned in the final Cixous quote. Your slippery *I* is exciting, the slippage between the mask of Nancy Drew and the speaker of this collection. You say, "…we slip in and out of each other." Can you tell us a little about your use of *I* here, how it relates to the mask of persona, between the self and Nancy?

First, Sara, a thousand thank yous to you and everyone at *Driftwood* for being such generous readers of this collection and shepherding it into the world so carefully.

In this collection, I think the *I* is one of the many ghosts that weave through it. Even poems without *I*'s have *I*'s hidden in the architecture; it is the consciousness through which the poem exists. I like to think of the *I* as the presence of intimacy, while, at the same time, I am aware of the way that trauma can make all sorts of *I*-ish realities unstable. Memory is fallible and it is also, for so many of us, the only sort of truth we have. If everything in this book is true then nothing in this book is true, because there is no way that, more than twenty years later, I can be accountable to the realities of 1999. So I sent Nancy to investigate. I surrendered *my I* to become *an I*, aware that she, bracketed and cut off from the rest of the text, could better attend to memory from a distance.

Less esoterically, we are all playing with personas all the time. The persona poem can approach our biographical contradictions as material instead of fact.

Everything is persona, it seems. This is something I think about often in my own work: perhaps everything is a mask. It's what draws me in, the shakiness and layers of my own identity, of cultural identity. Have you, also, always been drawn to the persona poem as form? Do you have any advice for readers who might want to explore persona farther (or write their own)?

I have! I love the persona poem. One of the first collections of poetry I ever read—actually, the same time as when the things in *Girlhood x a Haunting* took place—was Denise Duhamel's *Kinky*, which is a book of persona poems written from the perspective of different Barbie dolls. Then a million years later, my first collection of poems explores queer feminist themes through personas of the Voyager Space Probes. I didn't set out for *Girlhood* to be a persona driven project, but the material of the persona itself became the material of the collection.

I think when they're best used, persona poems allow poets to imagine into the more tender parts of their own personalities and explore them through a different lens. That's the project: becoming more of who we are. Not to imagine ourselves into other people or histories that aren't our own.

People always want to label things. If you use *I*, you're suddenly a confessional poet. As a woman poet, I've occasionally been called confessional in a derogatory way, but I believe in confession, in the complicated history of confessional poetry, and that those writers called confessional have often been underestimated. What is your take on confessional as a label? Do you see this book fitting into that history of confession?

I'm also always thinking about the label of confessional! People lobbing it as a misogynist insult always betray their lack of understanding of American poetics. Like, sure, please compare me to Plath. I'm not going to get mad about it.

Whether this collection is or not… in the most semantic sense, I would argue, no, it isn't. Rosenthal coined the term "confessional" to draw a distinction between poems that he felt masked biographical material and poems that, as he read them, didn't. This project is deeply concerned with the viability of those masks.

This feels deeply connected to the authoritative use of your own name. There's power in naming. It reminds me of what Claudia Cortese did in *Wasp Queen*, blending the self into a character, which could also be another mask. How did you come to the choice to use your own name vs. aliases like Hannah, or simply continuing the Nancies?

I love that you mention *Wasp Queen*—I adore that book and definitely see my Nancy in conversation with Claudia's Lucy (even though I don't think Lucy would like Nancy very much).

I wrote the first draft of this book in early 2016; I'm writing the answers to these questions in 2024. Any answer I give here will be inaccurate—while also the closest thing I have to the truth. The book in a nutshell! With that in mind, what I remember is this:

I think that the first line I wrote for the project was "I tell people more than they need to know." But no, that's too close. Too precious. Too much like salt in the wound.

I revised it to "Jessica tells people more than they need to know."

I think I wrote on like that for a few pages when I decided/realized/understood—however it is that creative knowledge comes into being!—Jessica would pretend to be Nancy Drew in order to attend to the mysteries at hand. I, however, do everything to extremes.

All of this process is to say that the question of naming was immediately a key question. I knew that I wanted to take my name back from the mouths that weren't mine. I also knew there were things I didn't want to name; a close reader will notice that I don't name the nature of abuse.

In the collection, Hannah is always in reference to my stepmother. She was my father's accomplice as much as she was abused by him; all things are complicated. Nancy's friends come into play for a couple of reasons, but one is because I love the way that a shift in friend-group signalizes a shift in an understanding of one's own identity.

I love that idea of taking back your name, but also creating more distance by writing in the third person. How did you decide when to use Jessica and when to use *I*?

I love this question because "Jessica" appears maybe seven times across the 90ish pages of this collection. She's become a ghost haunting her own text! Or, maybe, I've become a ghost haunting my own text. More likely, I've become a ghost haunting hers. Either way, I'm obsessed. Boo!

"Jessica" appears in the text in the moments when the world between Jessica and Nancy are at their thinnest: a clue, a dream, and a diversion into premise. It's the moments when the two realities collide.

Heiber and Janes, in their nonfiction book, *A Haunted History of Invisible Women: True Stories of America's Ghosts*, explore how most famous American ghosts are silenced and abused or powerless women. Was this element of spectrality on your mind as you wrote this?

Definitely, yes. I also think there is a whole host of abuses which aren't given names because they "aren't that bad" compared to other horrors. I did that to myself for a long time.

Also, speaking of women ghosts! I think most people know that Carolyn Keene was a persona that masked a whole series of ghostwriters. The two most notable were Mildred Benson and Harriet Stratemeyer Adams. Mildred Benson wrote most of the initial run of Nancy Drew; these aren't the yellow books that I grew up with, but longer, blue books. Benson was given the outlines for each book from Edward Stratemeyer's *Stratemeyer Syndicate*—the same house that published *The Hardy Boys* and other dime store series from the era. The first edition of the blue *The Secret of the Old Clock* was published in 1930. Later, in 1957, after her father had died, Harriet Stratemeyer Adams rewrote the series with a whole other group of ghost writers. So, we have these books that were written (predominantly) by one ghost and edited by another. There were about nine authors of the early books in total. Matryoshka dolls of authorship.

Wow! I really did not realize how many ghostly layers exist in Nancy Drew. Were there significant differences you found between the ghost-

writers which inspired you? Do you see this book joining that stack of dolls, in some way?

When I started the project, I knew that the books had been ghostwritten and was puzzling through the implications of that for a twenty-first century queer feminist poetic. What does it mean to have a man put your voice into the mouth of another woman? What does it mean to get paid a flat rate to write a novel that will never see your name on it but, instead, be attached to a person who doesn't—and has never—existed? How does that ventriliquism complicate our notion or understanding of authorship?

To keep tugging at this metaphor, I hope that this book can play in the same dollhouse as the Matryoshka dolls, or maybe wave from across the street, but this isn't a *Nancy Drew* book. She's the magnifying glass as much as she's the girl holding it.

Is Nancy Drew a spectral force for your speaker, and beyond that, for all American girls? Is there something she represents about American girlhood, or girlhood in general, that you wanted to make clear for your readers?

I think Nancy Drew is, in many ways, a cipher for middle-class white feminism. She is constantly attempting to solve other people's problems while also engaging in a deep othering of people who do not fit into a WASP aesthetic. Villains are frequently "swarthy" immigrants who are attempting to steal from old-monied people who are just "temporarily" down on their luck. Nancy makes it her job to protect whiteness, even—or especially!—at her own expense.

How much research into (or rereading of!) Nancy Drew did you do while writing this?

So much. So very much. Along with reading the books, I read a fair bit of literary criticism exploring queer possibilities and class consciousness across the span of the *Nancy Drew Mystery Novels*, as well as studies of the Stratemeyer Syndicate.

I think I might be in the last generation of girls who grew up reading the yellow spine *Nancy Drew* books. Re-reading them as an adult, there were two things that struck me that I didn't realize as a kid (how could I have?). The first is that my family didn't resemble the Drews—more often than not, it resembled the villains. The second is that in almost every book Nancy is drugged, beaten, kidnapped, assaulted, or left for dead. For all the things that she's preternaturally good at, the most important is survival.

What would you like your readers to take away from this deeply rooted cultural depiction, this survivor/cipher, and her legacy?

When you think about how much violence she experiences, there's something very surreal about Nancy's cultural position as a compass point for plucky, self-started, young womanhood. For, in a lot of ways, freedom. How many of us have stories that we heard from our mothers, grandmothers, aunts, whoever, about the incredibly normalized violence they experienced? The matter-of-factness of it all? There's not that much difference between Nancy Drew and, oh, Laura Palmer. Nancy is a cultural artifact from a dying world. Let it die.

Stylistically, tell us about the graphic elements of this collection (your use of the eye, pencil, photographs, etc., the white space, and even upside-down text). Where did the choice to include more visual elements come from, for you, and how do you think visual elements can complement text?

Most of the visual elements were included to create a sense of disorientation. I am, perhaps, too attached to mimetic gestures, but I love it when the text enacts its own content in curious or surprising ways.

The eye was the first graphic to enter the pages. I was curious about the way that it both represented being surveilled and surveillance, as well as the trope of the evil eye. Are you the one looking or the one being looked at? Is there a difference? I think that's always a question in this book. The chart of definitions of the word "pen" on page five gestures towards some of this tension.

Each *Nancy Drew* book includes drawings of key scenes from the books coupled with a pull quote. In many ways, I wanted the book to look and feel as much like a yellow covered *Nancy Drew* book as I could in order to create a—hopefully—productive tension surrounding the artifice of it all.

Tell me more about "mimetic gestures," your attachment and usage!

I'm just such a sucker for materiality in that way! It might be a ghost of formalism. In this collection, it's part of why so many of the pieces are written in such a squared off prose block. I needed there to be something really standardized for things to not only rebel against, but find order within.

I'd love to also hear about how you see the bracket functioning, in your poetry. Are there any poets using punctuation in similar or interesting ways who inspired you to experiment visually, or anyone you would recommend to our readers who are interested in reading more work like yours?

I hope that the bracket cues to a different type of interiority. A type of window that the *I* is peering out of, watching the unfolding, and trying to understand where she fits into the narrative of her own life. Isn't this one of the great questions of girlhood?

Inspiration! So much! Poets are nothing if not the community we write within. This list will be woefully inadequate. I already mentioned Claudia's book above, and I would point any reader who wants to think more about the grammar of queer femme desire to Rae Gouriand's work. I read so much of Kim Hyesoon's work in translation while composing this project, and Mei-mei Berssenbrugge's collaborations with Kiki Smith were incredibly important to me in thinking about the relationship between poems and visual text. Danielle Pafunda's *Dead Girls Speak in Unison* and Alice Notley's *Descent of Alette* both were compasses, in very different ways, for thinking about vocality. *Beast Meridian* by Vanessa Angélica Villarreal helped me think about the field of the page in different ways. Brenda Hillman, of course. This list could go on forever.

Many of these are untitled (until we get to "The Rescue" on page 23, in fact!), and it makes me think of Melissa Crowe's book *Lo*, which contains a long poem in which childhood sexual abuse is presented in a fragmented, unyielding way, which feels like how traumatic memory works, circling back to memory. In a 2023 AWP panel on the long poem, she and panelists described it as such, going into the history of the long poem as a primarily male form. Did you intend for this to read as a series of long poems? If so, what is your take on inserting such distinctly female voice and trauma into that form?

At times I think of this as a book length poem. At other times, an auto-fiction in verse. Others, an affective memoir. I hope that it is slippery.

I am hardly an expert, but I will talk about Enheduanna as long as anyone lets me. She was a Sumerian priestess to Inanna who is also recognized, at this point, as the first named author. Her poem is an epic account of the mythology of the goddess Inanna, following her through her full descent and ascent cycles. I won't pretend that there isn't a misogynist literary tradition intent on upholding the mythos of long poems as somehow belonging to male voices, nor an insidious history of the erasure of women's voices through both literary and capitalist impulses, but I do know that as long as there has been writing there have been women and gender-nonconforming people writing long poems.

There is painful trauma here that is addressed in such an artful way. What advice do you have for our readers about how to enter difficult spaces like this, both as readers and as fellow writers?

For writers, I can only say, *be gentle with yourself*. So many of us have had our boundaries violated so many times in such horrible ways—you don't owe anyone access to your trauma, and whatever way you choose to talk (or not!) talk about it is completely valid. Can editing be a reparative gesture? A spell for understanding where the story ends and where I begin? I feel so. I think so. I hope so.

For readers? At some point, you will read someone's story and feel like you are entitled to more than they have given. You aren't. The sense that you are, however, is one worth interrogating. It can only teach you more about yourself.

NOTES

Italicized material & chapter titles are drawn from the following *Nancy Drew Mystery Stories*:

The Secret of the Old Clock, Grosset & Dunlap, 1959
The Bungalow Mystery, Grosset & Dunlap, 1960
The Secret of Red Gate Farm, Grosset & Dunlap, 1961
Password to Larkspur Lane, Grosset & Dunlap, 1966

Quotations in "FOLLOWING A CLUE" are from the following films:

The Godfather, Francis Ford Coppola, Paramount Pictures, 1972
The Goodfellas, Martin Scorcese, Warner Brothers, 1990
Scarface, Brian De Palma, Universal Pictures, 1983
Saturday Night Fever, John Badham, Paramount Pictures, 1977

Epigraph quotes are from the following books:

Lucie Brock Broido, "A Girl Ago," *Stay, Illusion* (*Alfred A. Knoph*, 2013)
Bobbie Anne Mason, *The Girl Sleuth* (*University of Georgia Press*, 1995)
Helene Cixous, translated by Betsy Wing, *The Book of Promethea* (*University of Nebraska Press,* 1991)

Definitions on page five inspired by the entry for "pen" in *Merriam Webster* (Merriam-Webster.com).

ACKNOWLEDGEMENTS

"A Forgotten Secret" *Poem a Day*, January 9, 2020 (published as "Did Rise")
"Helpful Disclosures" *Third Coast*, 2018 (published as "One Need Not be a Chamber to be Haunted"
"An Unexpected Adventure," "A Missing Will," "Strange Instructions," "The Angry Dog," "Nancy's Risky Undertaking," "A Suspenseful Search," and the untitled piece on page 9, *Black Warrior Review*, 2018.

Thank you to the editors of those journals for their generosity and care.

GRATITUDE

Thank you to my friends and colleagues at the University of Utah who provided feedback on the earlier versions of this project, especially Jacqueline Osherow, Katharine Coles, Melanie Rae Thon, Michelle MacFarlane, Jenny Andrus, Disa Gambera, Molly Gaudry, Ray Levy, Susannah Nevison, Evie Atkinson, Paula Jane Mendoza, Michelle McFarlane, Michelle Donohue, Cori Anne Winrock, Noam Dorr, Jason Daniels, JP Grasser, Zack Medlin, and Joe Sacksteder.

Thank you Hedgebrook and the Taft-Nicholson Center for the time, space, and care necessary to complete this collection.

Thank you so, so much to Sara Moore Wagner and James McNulty and everyone at *Driftwood* for making the sweetest home for this weird and vulnerable project.

Thank you to my families of poetry and magic, especially Brent Armendinger, EJ Colen, Rae Gouriand, Janine Kovac, Rae Meads, Elae Moss, Derek Robbins, Emily Sketch Haines, & Monica Street. Thank you to the Flying Flounders for the daily deepening during the quietest time. Thank you to the community at Y-WE Write for dreaming new possibilities of girlhood. Thank you, Rollin. Thank you Karina, Molly, Courtney, Claire P., Skye, and Tracy. Thank you Melanie Frazza, Rosalia Wehr, Lucas Kade, Julia Chille, Monica Berini, Dharma Dailey, Carrie Lanza, Brook Gillian, Maria Molteni, and all the MACARONIS imagining ways of healing in community.

Thank you to the me who survived.
Thank you to the me who didn't.
I love you.

Thank you forever and ever, Claire Scott. None of this would be possible without you.

Girlhood x A Haunting was completed on the lands of the Duwamish People, the Coast Salish People, the Ute People, and the Northern Shoshone People. Thank you.

Photography by Laura Brooks Photography

Jessica Rae Bergamino is the author of *UNMANNED* (*Noemi Press*, 2018) as well as chapbooks from *dancing girl press* and *Sundress Publications*. She lives in Seattle, Washington.

MORE TITLES FROM
DRIFTWOOD PRESS

comics, fiction, poetry
chapbooks & collections

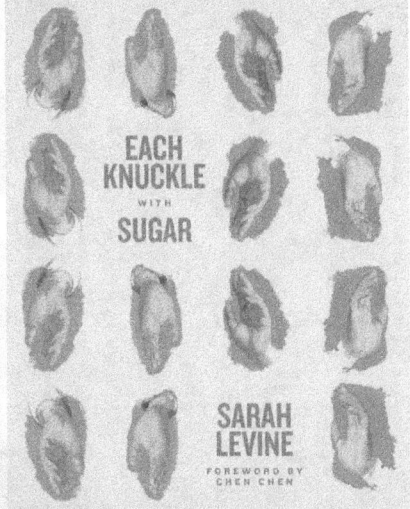
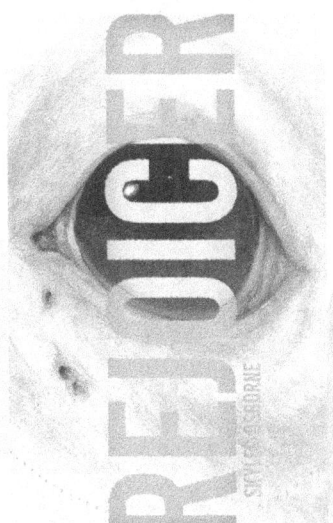

www.ingramcontent.com/pod-product-compliance
Lightning Source LLC
Chambersburg PA
CBHW081433070526
44586CB00020B/2574